# SPILT MILK

# SPILT MILK

SARAH MAGUIRE

*Secker & Warburg*
POETRY

First published in Great Britain 1991 by
Martin Secker & Warburg Limited
Michelin House, 81 Fulham Road,
London SW3 6RB

A CIP catalogue record for this book
is available from the British Library

ISBN 0 436 27095 1

Printed in Great Britain by
St Edmundsbury Press Limited,
Bury St Edmunds, Suffolk

FOR CRISPIN: HIS BOOK

# CONTENTS

# ACKNOWLEDGEMENTS

Acknowledgements are due to the following:

*Landfall, London Review of Books, New Chatto Poets: Number Two* (London, 1989), *Poetry Now, Times Literary Supplement, Verse*.

'The Fall' won a minor prize in the 1985 National Poetry Competition; 'The Divorce Referendum' received a special commendation in the 1987 Arvon Foundation International Poetry Competition.

Having been prevented by reasons of gender from visiting Mount Athos, my account of the isthmus and its history in 'The Garden of the Virgin' is dependent on many sources, notably P. Sherrard's *Athos: The Holy Mountain* (London, 1982) and the enthusiastic research of Crispin Hughes and Níall McLaughlin.

# MAY DAY, 1986

*for Tadeusz Sławek*

Yesterday, the weather in Warsaw
was the same as London's: *Sunny, 18°*
(*sixty-four Fahrenheit*). I am sitting
in a walled garden drinking gin,
the fading sky as blue as this tonic water
loosening its bubbles against the flat ice.

What is in the air? The first midges;
a television three doors down, its hum
like this lone bat avoiding the walnut tree.
A dog barks. In other houses lights come on –
the street an Advent Calendar opening
its doors. This house is in darkness,

its seven windows admitting the night.
I'm trying to read *Mansfield Park*, to learn
how Fanny finds love and a mansion
through keeping silence. All week
the weather report has plotted the wind
leaving Chernobyl with its freight

of fall-out: cancer settling on Poland –
the radio-activity an inaudible fizz
in the cells, rupturing thorax or liver,
the intimacy of the bowel. They say it won't
reach here. I stare at the sky till all
I can see are the dead cells of my eyes,

jumping and falling. It's too dark to read –
only the flare of a late *Kerria japonica*,
trained to the wall. I think of your letter
in my drawer with the handkerchiefs,
one page torn by an earlier reader. Socrates
distrusted writing, its distance from

the grain of the voice. I come indoors
to write you all the things I couldn't say
a year ago. Later, on the news, they will show
gallons of contaminated Polish milk
swilled into sewage, a boy crying
at the sting of iodine he must swallow

against the uncertain air.

# PERFECT TIMING

The night I fell in love with you I lost my watch:
stripping off at the sea's edge, it fell into the dark
as I swam out into a night thick with stars,
with fishermen calling from one lit boat to another
of their catches and harbours, leaving for the dawn.
Imagine it now, plunged deep in cool sand, still hidden
years later, grains ticking over it one by one –
as your hands slide into me and I move to their pulse.

# BED AND BREAKFAST

We have booked into a hotel room so hot
it is another cliché. We are exhumed on this great bed,
a wedding present to an ugliest daughter.
A yellow street lamp shows the grain of your skin,
the small hairs puckered round your nipples.
The couple in the next room are in love.
Our tooth-glass chink-chinks on its stand in sympathy.

# UISGE BEATHA

Such a glutton for pleasure. Absorbed on your sofa
I watch this fire, its heat, its mutations.
Your keen knife slips into the flesh of an orange
and a cacophony of Os ravels into your lap, unbroken.

Not for years – but I'm too late: already
you're spanning my wrist, have taken my arm
right up to the elbow. Then the stem of my glass.
What do I remember? – a litany of whiskies:

Lagavulin, Laphroaig, Talisker, Aberlour,
The Macallan – the hot sweet smoked malt
that I burned of and for you. Or your exact,
fluent fingers. The perfume near your throat.

And how I dreamt of that house with red doors,
a huge garden, and two weeping willows.
A cool brook I'd fall into and not wish to leave.

The edge of Tunisia is like the sea-side
or an abandoned set from *Beau Geste*.
It is one hundred and ten degrees.
You eat pilchards on Ryvita
and long for a sorbet
or the beginnings
of a pier.

By the time you reach the Tademait Plateau
all the hairs on your body are bleached
to the last shade of straw. Here even
your shit is a landmark. Heat bends
the horizon of ochre and orange
under a muscular sky.

Near Tamanrasset you find a spring of fresh
fizzy water. Plunging your arms into
this cold spawn you feel its gases
tick along your wrists.

The Hoggar Mountains are white on your map,
their lavas stunned into gothic bosses
and sills – cathedrals without relics
or candlesticks. You cup your palm
round an elbow of basalt and
search for your echo.

Then you meet a hermit carrying a gas-cylinder.
For thirty years he has lived where no one
has lived, among lava and stars. His
plastic sandals are beginning
to give at the heel.

Pause in the *feche-feche* and you drown.
On your right is a blue *deux-chevaux*
up to its knees. Then the emptied
suitcase and one sling-back shoe
losing its grip.

Each night you sleep out under a big sky
and watch the North Star slip out of
reach. You envy the confident moon
intent upon leaving.

At three o'clock the night loosens its stars like
spilt salt. How you long for one to lighten
your tongue like a line of lemon sherbet
or a eucharist you could take and tuck
behind your teeth.

Eighty miles from Agadez you unscrew the last can
of spring water. You hear the dim hiss of
one thousand miles north. Small bubbles
freckle your mouth.

For some years he still would harden as he
Pushed his fingers through my stubbly hair,
Then gathering my small breasts in his fists
Would bite them, murmuring of a glorious fruit
He'd tasted once in Singapore.
                                    At twenty
He'd impressed me with his rooms large enough
To run in, with his nonchalance for glass,
With the books he'd hold but never open.
There was the gift of his cool hands along
My shoulder blades, of the olives he'd split
And stone: pressing their charcoal flesh against
My tongue, *These taste of you*, he whispered, once.
In his absence I'd wait all day in the orchard
Longing for his fruit to fall. Still innocent
And pre-Newtonian I'd lie beneath the *Worcester
Pearmain* watching the sour fruits soften to rot.
He'd spend entire weekends training his beloved
Nectarines and damsons, cherries, apricots
And pears – the reluctant he'd hard-prune back,
Or whip-graft their rootstocks.
                                    The day I left
I watched him nail his favoured espalier apple,
Arm by arm, against a reddened wall.

# SPILT MILK

Two soluble aspirins spore in this glass, their mycelia
fruiting the water, which I twist into milkiness.
The whole world seems to slide into the drain by my window.

It has rained and rained since you left, the streets black
and muscled with water. Out of pain and exhaustion you came
into my mouth, covering my tongue with your good and
    bitter milk.

Now I find you have cashed that cheque. I imagine you
slipping the paper under steel and glass. I sit here in a circle
of lamplight, studying women of nine hundred years past.

My hand moves into darkness as I write, *The adulterous woman
lost her nose and ears; the man was fined.* I drain the glass.
I still want to return to that hotel room by the station

to hear all night the goods trains coming and leaving.

# STILL AT SEA

Each night you returned
to the Mediterranean
just touching Marsala

and would dream of the sea
repeating itself,
the light slivering

all over your ceiling.
Each night you woke
with his back humped

against yours, his fists
gripping the pillows,
as he dreamt of his cargoes

packed in dry docks,
or of the Caspian Sea
locked into itself.

Then, after half a life,
you left his house
full of maps and dust

and found your paints
in thirteen shades
of cobalt blue and jade.

In Cefalù your dream
became your home:
a house on the harbour

where the sea slapped
at your walls.
Standing in the kitchen,

up to your elbows
in underwear and soap,
you would look out

to find the waves
organising the pebbles,
scouring the rocks.

At night, alone
with the moonlight
and a smallish grappa,

you pictured yourself
as a Cubist sacrifice:
sectioned in monochrome,

your lap full of triangles,
the moon shifting
her perspectives

to whiten your ankles,
throw your mouth into
doubt. You occupied

that house nine months –
watching the seasons,
then the tourists,

come and go. Each morning
there was coffee and
fresh foccaccia by the sea,

then the market for
your aubergines and fennel,
or that blue and silver

banded fish; once home
you'd take a knife and slit
it up the belly to reveal

the sack of wasted eggs,
the liver, then the tiny heart:
its carmine blood

releasing the grain
of your scrubbed deal table
and its memories of leaves.

Three years' silence
and I wonder
if you're still at sea.

I spread out
all your letters on my desk
to plot your travels:

they're full of water-colours –
mostly harbours,
reaching out to light.

The very last
tells how you found
the cigarette machine

outside your door split
by a bullet-hole,
its fractured glass

like the sun a child might draw
on the edge of a tablecloth.
There was no blood

to be seen: only the smell
of washed stone,
and a woman with a bucket

slipping out of view.

# PORCELAIN

My house was so damaged by frost
That odd parcels of stucco would fissure
Then fall, rupturing on the pavement.
This spring the scaffold mounts, joist
By plank, a mantis hugging the plaster.
I hid today in my sightless bathroom
And felt the meniscus on the cold tap
Form and split, fill and burst,
The yellowing porcelain seeping to rust.

# MORPHOLOGY

At a quarter-past-three
the bottom shelf gave up,
casting its yellowed magazines
and tampons to the floor –
and that marble egg
which split in two,
revealed itself
as thickened marble,
pink and veined with
dirty cream, all through.
I long for a geode –
some simple rock
that would admit a heart
of amethyst or malachite –
or that pebble
which you found in Brighton,
an ammonite:
the intricacies and volumes
of its life
expressed as a skeleton,
worn in stone.

# A FORMAL GARDEN

*The bourgeois fate: to eat without hunger, mate without desire.*
                                        Nadine Gordimer

I came to from that dream
Stuccoed with sweat –
In it I'd designed a french window
That was fashioned from
The skinned limbs of my daughter.
Gradually I became soothed
By the machinery of cleaning,
By the sound of my crockery
Being rinsed and stacked.
I became identified by choice
Coffees, by my impeccable
Taste for myself.

I love to gaze through the glass
At my walled, formal garden
With its finest York stone,
And small, precise topiaries
Of box and yew, the gravel
Raked into line. I have studied
The morphologies of phloem and xylem,
And can plot the progress of sugars
Changing light into ferns,
Or the aetiology of a fungus
Bulking through a rose
To block out its heart.

My wife left years ago:
For a while I was trapped
In the comfort of nostalgia

Till I burnt all the books
And silks she abandoned,
Then moved. Now, almost daily,
I rise from my blueprints
Only to find that buildings crumple
Like children's skulls:
The cladding flayed back,
The joists exposed
In a bitter, corrosive grin.

# RIME

In a street full of houses
yours is a lone moon.

It gleams under tungsten lamps,
one corner of plaster just

peeling. Its huge windows are
craters, fathomless.

I come all elbows and restraint,
fearful of crockery. The food

is boiled twice. Stillborn
vegetables clack in my throat.

One night I stayed. Opening
room after room of a lost set,

each photographically still.
I slept in the smallest.

Its sealed window held a garden
stiffened with frost.

# DRY RUN

Tonight the clocks go back. It is three weeks since you left.
I read through all your letters, then hid them
next to the bundle of ten years past.
Nobody knows what Martha did
when Lazarus died again.

# THE GARDEN OF THE VIRGIN

*In the Gospel of the Egyptians . . . the Saviour himself said,*
I am come to destroy the works of the female.
　　　　　　Clement of Alexandria, *Stromateis*, Book III

### I

Fearing the approach of his second death,
Lazarus – he who had known the chill
of the tomb, who had felt the soft worms
weld to his flesh – Lazarus, the Bishop of Cyprus,
requested the Virgin's blessing. He sent
a boat for her, and Mary sailed from the coast
of Palestine – the clear sky big with itself,
the sea blue as the sky – till a storm drove
her off course, and she came upon her garden.

From the far northern coast
of Greece, from the low
treeless shore of Halkidiki,
three arms of land slide into
        the Aegean Sea.

From the edge of the third
Mount Athos pierces the sky,
its darkening, gashed
escarpments finished by
        a crest of white.

Below, the isthmus falls away,
its rough spine a wood as dense
as any fairy-tale, as thick
with wolves. The forest of Athos
        is pungent

with the gums and oils of pine,
of juniper and thuja, is massed
with ilex and arbutus,
with the loose mauve flowers
        of the Judas tree.

III

At Clementos, Mary
alighted
into recognition.
The Pagans fled.

In their makeshift
shrines, the idols
of their female gods
debased themselves

before her, imploding
into dust. The Virgin
walked through Athos
in the cool of evening,

inhaling its aromas,
gathering the blooms
of oleander and hibiscus.
She declared this garden

her domain, declared
(recalling Eve)
no other female
should come to foul

this paradise.
Then she left for Cyprus,
for the final death
of Lazarus.

The monks who came to cultivate
the Virgin's garden
obeyed her law.

St Theodosius the Studite wrote:
*Keep no female animal*
*for use in house or field.*

*The holy fathers*
*never used such –*
*nor does nature need them.*

Ewelambs and their ewes
were slaughtered. Cows
butchered. Heifers slain.

The sow, the gilt
and the nanny goat:
all dead and banned.

Bitches murdered one
by one. Each hen
felt the press of thumbs

about her throat, the neck
snapped taut – and then
the slump. Each egg

was gathered up, each eggshell
crumpled in a viscid mess of yolk,
thrown oozing down the cliffs,

where, boiling in the waves,
it made a salty broth
the gulls sucked up.

Only the cats stayed on:
the cats to catch the rats
that dropped their young

despite the monks,
despite the Virgin's stern
injunction. At night

it was the cats
who ran the place:
softening the hands and throats

of anchorites and cenobites,
their lithe fur
soothing the flesh made stiff

through deprivation.
And at night the wolves
roamed yowling

through the Virgin's garden:
the sole beast
with cunning enough

to breach the fine neck
of the isthmus.
Miles up, alone

in his stone cottage,
reached only by chains
hung over cliffs,

a hermit wakes up, sodden
from a lycanthropic nightmare,
with his hair

on end. He had sensed
the slow breath
of the wolf, had stared

deep into her lemon eyes,
as still as oil
or candelight, then

felt himself run off with her –
feral, hirsute, opening out his lungs
to greet the moon.

# FOREIGN LABOUR

## I

I imagine rain the only atmosphere
staining the habits of some rented room
where you're perched, thinly, in a shifting town,
your labour redundant.

How you'd smooth your frail hands
and remember dances that have cost a sea and friendship.
Dusk buckles the room and you're lost in the gas hiss,
deaf to the cars, as a meter clicks your food away.

## II

She slept soundly in the chest of drawers,
but they took your daughter and the clothes you'd made.
So you go home to Dublin, its rains and puckered laws.
That climate starves you. Then you meet again

and leave for Liverpool, a ghetto
and a second child.

# THE FRACTURE CLINIC

The weather broke the day my parents met me:
after an early spring the air turned hard; drizzle;

the gutters blocked with blossoms of the palest pink.
They climbed the big stairs to the Priest's house

in St Charles Square, and found me silent in a cot.
Then they named me, took me from a Home to *home*.

At twenty-one I found the mother I had never known,
much smaller than I'd thought, her hands like mine.

*Too much dancing*, she told me. Saturday nights
she'd sneak out the back, her black pumps in a paper bag,

and take the bus to town. One night in June,
with all of Dublin lit up, spread beneath her, she fell

pregnant, then lost me in West London to the Church.
Last Saturday I danced too much and fell.

They have taken me to St Charles Hospital
where I drowned in anaesthesia: beneath a star-shaped atrium

I watched the milky light turn crystalline, then I went
under. Now I'm lying in Recovery,

my wrist encircled by my date of birth, my postcode
and my name, all written upside down.

# PSORIASIS

At five-and-a-half the skin on my knees
turned to paper and flaked off.
I would peel away the scales
and lay them on the window-sill –
each a milky carapace fretted with pores.
It was still light. I could hear
the older children hiding
and finding each other again.
I put all my toys in the bed
and slept on the floor.

No-one went out now.
My father's hip-bone was crumbling away.
They had taken him to the hospital
and opened it up like an egg;
at its core was an abscess
the doctor plucked out.
One afternoon I watched him asleep,
his hands gathering the eiderdown.

My mother was frightened.
*I get on a bus and I just can't breathe.*
When I broke the tea-cup she locked
herself in the bathroom for hours.
I squeezed under my bed
and traced its paisley mattress
with my finger – the swirls and flowers
fell into themselves, repeating
and repeating into the dark.
I wondered where the pattern began.

# A FAMILY HOLIDAY

Most of all he hated the Irish – *Papists the lot of them*;
my grandfather spat in the grate. My father was in the scullery
trying to whistle, or fingering the willow-pattern cups.
He hung a tea-towel to dry on the back of a chair
and tapped the barometer.

*You must eat your grandad's food*, my mother hissed.
In the cut-glass bowl the raspberries moved – maggots.
I covered them with a fist of sugar, watched it
haemorrhage to a juice thick as the tears of martyrs.
The cream, a blent river, turned pink.

My father and I waited in the graveyard. We could hear
my mother singing slightly off-key, my grandfather
pressing the organ. My father sighed, then spread *The Universe*
across a Methodist grave. His bottle of Guinness
left Os by a photograph of the Pope.

That night my window slammed and shuddered with the rain.
The sky was mustard, then alight. I counted three elephants
between the lightning and the crash. A group of children
ran in jerks beside the river; struck by lightning,
one became a Catherine wheel, staggered, and went out.

*I'll take her for a walk to the farm*. My father leaned
over the gate and waved till he was small. My grandfather said
I must help him empty the mole-traps. He tossed one at me.
It's neck was floppy and one eye had burst. I took its hand
in mine – pink, smaller than a doll's.

# THE DIVORCE REFERENDUM

Here it's a fortnight to Carnival.
On hot nights I lie outside the sheets, listening to
the steel-bands practising till dawn – the throats

of oil-drums beaten to chromatics, glistening in the dark.
When it rains the railway seems to move
up the street – train after train slipping westwards

from Paddington, thickening the night.
You left from platform three. I leaned over the barrier,
my hands pressed together as if in prayer.

When you rang I was still wet from the bath. After ten years
silence you realise how you love me. I touch you
and a vessel in your feminine nose gives way –

blood and your salt-sweet tears flood my fingers and lips.
Later my own blood inscribes the fresh sheets –
the scarlet letter, a map of desire nothing can shift.

In three months you'll leave Dublin. You tell me
the Divorce Referendum has made you choose exile.
In Camden Town you weigh a pint of Guinness in your palm,

drain it, push away the glass. I trace the rings
of beer-stains on the table with my finger,
or smoke your cigarettes right down to the stub.

Somewhere between here and Dún Laoghaire the boat broke
     down.
For hours you drift in the eye of your storm.
Leaning from a railing into stillness

you watch the amber light of the ferry fall into the night,
your eyes stinging from their search for a harbour.
Later you will write, *Perhaps I am still at sea.*

On the phone your voice is sallow with exhaustion,
its timbre frayed by a line carried miles under water.
When your daughter calls out in her sleep you must leave

to comfort her. I'll lie here now till dawn, twisting
the phone-cord round my fingers till my nails turn white,
longing for suffrage, for your casting vote.

# MOVING HOME

You're emptying the trunks;
one by one they slide down from the loft:
fat coffins, furred over with dust.

The third reveals the girl
you might have been: browned snap-shots
of you squinting in the sun,

one hand holding his, the other
nervous with a cigarette. Here are the letters
that you've never dared to read;

then buried under them you find the dress
he sent you from the States, of crimson watered silk.
You ease it from its chrysalis

of cellophane, and inhale the stiff aroma
of new cloth – as if you would throw off
those hard-worn rings, and leave.

# A CHERRY TREE

I have entered that domestic season –
Mending small china;
Sifting grains into cleansed jam-jars
And storing them, labelled, in darkness.

I wait alone in huge rooms
Listening to the hiss of cars passing.
In my garden stands a cherry tree,
Livid with rain.

# MEDIUM TO FINE-GRAINED VESICULAR CRYSTALLINE ROCK OF IGNEOUS ORIGIN, & CONCRETE

When I was twelve men landed on the moon. Awake till dawn,
I watched the TV with the sound turned down
show pictures of Michelin Men,
light-headed,

fumbling over rocks: their masks of glassy black reflecting
back the moon, the gleaming moonscape yawning
into darkness – and at its edge
the sickle earth

veined with clouds and oceans, the two man-made walls
you can see from outer space. Afterwards
I watched the moon slide out of
my window:

she was still the same as yesterday, with half her face opened
to the night. A girl at school said, *You don't believe
they've been there? They filmed it all
in Hollywood.*

But then I saw the moon rock: just after Christmas I queued
for hours at the Geology Musueum to gaze at
a piece of the moon
so small

I could put it in my pocket. It lay under a huge curved dome
of glass, poised in silver tongs, each pore freckled
with crystals winking out at me.
All week

we've watched the break-up of Berlin: the Wall split open
by bulldozers and cranes, the patience
of a thousand chisels tapping
through the night.

And now you're back from Potsdamer Platz with your gift
of concrete: I hold the Berlin Wall
and feel its roughness
warm my hands.

November, 1989

# TACTICS

Soho is finished. You walk past a drunk
In a doorway sleeping with six plastic bags.
He wears one orange sock and no shoes.
So you take the last tube and then walk.
    Silence and the perfume of engines.
Somewhere a scream. Glass fractures.
Or the guttural taxis absorbed with leaving.
Then silence. All night. Once you heard
A child cry out in her sleep.
    You wake to a typewriter uncovered.
Light freezing the windows.
Like coming home to a dictated burglary.
Plants closed into themselves as before.
The carpet untouched. What is lost?
An address book? That sheaf of papers
You whispered to yesterday?
And you search but the place is unfingered.
    Some hour with no name. The fridge
Fallen silent. You waste in this
Permafrost kitchen. So white your teeth ache.
No redemption. No cigarettes either.
Soon will come buses. Sanity as big as
Elephants.

# LIMINAL

The fold-out map of Europe in my Filofax
has marked your town: a smudge on the grey line
limiting the blush-pink of Poland from a dull,
Czechoslovakian beige. Old maps of Poland lurch about,
or disappear: the disruptions of Silesia (its strikes
and its pollutants) once named as German. From a window
you strain to catch the border: two states meeting
on a bridge furred with barbed wire and lights,
the decorations of security.

We're out of touch again. You're grappling with
*The Origins of Geometry* or Nietzsche's styles:
'Supposing truth to be a woman'. . . . You've got your
*Spurs*. And I'm way back, pondering the significance
of the blush in novels full of fainting women.
In Edgeworth's *Belinda* a Mrs Freke, fond of whole-boots
and breeches, 'an expert marksman', petrifies
a young girl on the point of a rocking-stone
for the amusement of soldiers.

# FREUD IN PARIS

*To Charcot must be ascribed the most important influence in turning Freud from a neurologist into a psychopathologist.*
                                                        Ernest Jones

I  THE NEUROLOGIST DREAMS

Paris is frozen.
I live in a laboratory
walled with foetuses:
split buds of desire
pickled in glass.
Ebony and gaslight.
Moisture in rills
greases the dull windows.
And my tongue
in a bottle, floating.
I am one eye
condensed to a lens.
I lust for ganglia,
for the *Medulla oblongata*:
a tissue of tissues
unfolding. Accept
my slow knife.
Grant me annihilation
in the textures of velum.

Mecca.

God in his frock-coat
unleashes the demons.

The clockwork limbs –
an ecstasy of grace.

The numb skin
made palpable as fresh silk.

Tongues, pliant for wafers,
sing in six octaves

out of clacked wood.
Each wreck finds her storm's eye:

*Beach with me. Come.*
*A huge, mesmeric harbour beckons,*

*beckons in the candle*
*and the pocket watch.*

*I have no legs, Professor.*

He slid three pins
into her thigh. Miraculous.

Silver breaking through
clear skin, a fresh wax –

yet female with its blond down,
its neat stipple of pores.

He turned to smile at us: *Gentlemen* –
Then taken in his warm prayer,

his lulling, ticking nipple,
he bade her dance for us –

a pirouette of sinew and ankle
– till he clapped

and woke her into leglessness.

February. The city's filth refracts the spring.
The houses of the rich turn into themselves,
Jealous of warmth, of their light spilt onto snow.
Curtains and doors are slammed shut as I pass.
I am so homesick I could kneel down and weep here,
Loosening my tears into this kind snow –
Yet I am a man, a doctor – your future husband.
I have my new silk hat and gloves to think of.
How I hunger for the smallest comfort – to come home
Late at night to find you sleeping by our fire,
Your book slipped out of grasp, open on the floor.
Alone, I seek companionship in nerves and veins,
Dissecting desires and memories unfleshed.
(Martha, the *Medulla* has been your only rival.)
But this Charcot is a genius – he mesmerises
Chaos, draws law and method out of folly –
Hysteria is mathematical! Soon science will reduce
The twists of Goethe to a sum. I write this to you
From my desolate room. Above the roofs of distant homes
The dawn breaks and the pale stars climb.

# LUNATIC

We have sexed
A sterile rock rambling through a frigid night,
Relinquished wombs and cycles

To her span,
Made our receptacle for moods eccentric
To the shift of clocks.

Essentially
I am a tide, dependent on your flex and lapse –
A pendulum of blood.

And though obtuse
And punctual I wander through these rational streets –
Still some nights you heave

Silvered
Through this mottled glass, when I confess my gender
To your lucid gaze

And crave asylum in such lunacy.

# WHAT IS TRANSPARENT

The liquidity of glass: aeons from now
These panes will be a puddle on the floor.
Tonight I gaze through tricks and flaws
Which make the houses billow, the police van
On the corner monstrous – or a flick of black.

I hold the failed bulb to my ear and shake
Its filaments: still warm, it hardens in my palm.
In the winter of 'seventy-four we made love
By candle-light. After the strike the shops were
Glutted with candles: relics of fingers, sweating.

The miners are on strike again. I find two candles,
Turn out all the lights and watch the news:
The bluish screen tricking the faces of these men
Who work with darkness, underground.

You can always find him
slumped on the balcony of the Paradise Hotel
steadily drinking all the cold beers in town.

Here, night comes on quick:
the sky slipping from aubergine to black
between one swig and another,
the darkness filled with the drilling of insects.

Some nights he brings his servant along.
*Cowboy* he calls him, and pats his head –
*That gibberish* is beyond him.

A few beers later he peels back his sleeve
to display a tattooed lady;
then makes her breasts pout upwards
as he twists his wrist.

He's worked *The whiteman's grave*
since 'seventy-two,
a foreman out in Tarkwa mining gold.

The fierce heat underground was like a crucible:
he'll tell you how the Blacks
would sweat off seven pounds a shift.
Eight tons of ore was taken for each ounce of gold:

gouged out, crushed, then bleached with cyanide.
His gold is in his teeth,
small chinks glinting in the dark.

At two, his wife arrives to take him home.
She waits outside the bar,
smoothing down her frockcoat,
twisting the thin gold ring on her left hand.

*He's poisoning himself*, she whispers,
*losing all that weight from drink.*
And then the dermatitis:

his slackened, greyish skin is flaking off.
At four, he leaves his *Paradise*.
You watch him vanish in the darkness,
supported by his servant, followed by his wife.

# FALLING ORANGE

The clack of fresh walnuts tipped into a bowl,
or grapes split from the stem –

we could spit their pips as far as those lemon trees,
as high as your roof of bamboo and vines.

So you take two walnuts, edge to rim,
and press till they explode. Opening your fists

you offer their flesh, bitter and firm.
All night I felt the pull of the Mediterranean.

I would translate the small stars into consellations,
plot the fat moon falling orange into Naples.

# SMALL RAINS

After all these years
you still fracture my sleep:
I am lost in a cold bed,
my mouth wrought into bitterness.

I imagine you awake at this hour:
your cigarette starring the darkness,
lulled by the small rains
that settle on Dublin –

as I lean from a window
in a night with no moon
and watch the street lights
ebb into dawn.

# MUSHROOMS *À LA GREQUE*

Half-way through the washing-up
I wondered if I'd invented you.

All the places we made love
have been pulled down
or converted into something healthier.

I burnt your letters, lost the ring
and, you not being photogenic,
I own no out-of-focus Polaroids.

Even last night is down the drain.
The mushrooms *à la greque*
an irritation in the u-bend

or something stirring in the colon,
urgent for release.

# SKIP

Fridges sprout
on street corners,
a cubic fungus.

You plunder their magnets,
pod them from slit plastic
into my hands.

Like your shy gifts
of coat-hangers,
the cut-offs from carpets,

and those three stumps of marble:
a fractured table-top
became a frieze of ochre and rose –

you propped the sierra
against my door. Later
I opened my toe on it

and I watched you take
the wound in your mouth.
Grateful.

# FIN

## I

The last cigarette.
     My own blood, hissing
becomes rain at the windows.
     In a back room
a telephone rings, unanswered.

## II

Shark. Six-foot confounding the marble,
     gristle pointing the split neck.
By noon it had gone into steaks.
     The market fructified melons and mangoes.
Mange-tout.

     Later, one crate of snapper.
*I wouldn't bother with those, love*, he said,
     *they're all bone.*